F***
on the Ice Rink

SPICY
PUCK

ARIANA ST. CLAIRE

Version 09172023

Cover Image: Deposit Photos

Cover Design: Sarwah Creed

Formatting/Inner Images/Wrap: Dragonfly Graphic Designs

Editor: M.A. Patrick

Copy/Line Edit: Jasmine Acena

❀ Created with Vellum

For the Lucky Charms and Marshmallows that make the crazy moments perfectly imperfect with their love. And love us in our craziest moments even more...

And Mila, who gives us all the joy a little demon spawn could.

F*** On The Ice Rink is a 10 book collection series by Sarwah Creed, Wynter Ryan, Amanda Keen, Carolina Jax, Shannon O'Connor, Bonnie Poirier, Cassi Hart, Jenny Redford, Ariana St. Claire and Debbie Hope.

Grab your favorite book and get ready to melt on the ice. Don't miss out on this unforgettable series.

Triple Puck by Sarwah Creed
Three sizzling hockey stars leave me skating on thin ice!

Filthy Puck by Wynter Ryan
Will one filthy night be enough?

One Pucking Night by Amanda Keen
With everything to lose, can I risk trusting the man who once burned me…

That One Puck by Carolina Jax
Can a bit of honey sweeten the bad boy of hockey?

The Accidental Puck by Shannon O'Connor
One night of risks.

Naughty Puck by Bonnie Poirier
She's the spoiled little rich girl, he's the coach of the Harpsburg Rangers Hockey team.

Dirty Puck by Cassi Hart
Hockey is my nemesis.

Tasty Puck by Jenny Redford
No one frustrates her like her brother's best friend.

Spicy Puck by Ariana St. Claire

When the league's newest expansion team gets the one player she should stay away from, but she loves it when he watches her...

Even if her big brother is the coach of the team. And was his rival not too long ago.

Step Puck by Debbie Hope

My little stepsister, sexy, unattainable, walks back into my life.

Purchase all the books in the "F*** On The Ice Rink" series --- https://geni.us/FUnderTheRink2023

Thank you for being a part of our reading journey. We hope you enjoy these unforgettable stories as much as we enjoyed writing them. Your feedback means the world to us, so please consider leaving a review and sharing your thoughts with fellow readers.

Happy reading!

CHAPTER ONE

JULES

"*Y*ou're moving *where?*" I spun around in my tiny apartment, then dropped to my knees, searching under my bed for a little gray furball who thought it was hilarious to play hide and seek at only 9 weeks old.

All the while, my big brother, Max, kept talking as I struggled to keep my phone between my shoulder and ear.

"*We're* going to Seattle. And before you say no, hear me out, okay?"

I groaned as Daisy, my roommate and newly rescued best friend, tackled my wiggling fingers as she skittered out from under the dust ruffle. Her little claws tried to take me out, but she just wrapped her paws around my fingers and purred away. Stealing my heart all over again.

Wait, what??? I nearly dropped my phone. Oh, no, he didn't just say what I thought he did.

"Wait, did you say *we?* There is no we, Maxwell. I am not moving to Seattle! Pittsburgh is home. You knew when I moved here to be closer to you, that was the deal. No moving around," I protested with a giggle as Daisy nipped at me, her little engine purring loud for such a little creature.

"Jules, the Revenge don't want me as a player."

I sat up straight, scooping the kitten into my palm and cradling her against my chest. She snuggled against me, and my insides went all gooey marshmallow for her.

Silly kitten. Her purr reverberated through the phone as I shifted position, doing my best not to drop the phone or Daisy.

"What's that noise?"

I snorted. "Daisy."

"Who the hell is Daisy?"

"My roommate. And she doesn't want to move, either."

"Jules, since when do you have a roommate? Is it the rent? I thought I told you to call me if you needed-"

"She's a kitten, Max! I got a kitten. And she and I are happy here. Wait, did you say they didn't want you to play? What do they want you to do? Oh god, not the equipment manager! Do they know how horrible you are at keeping your equipment organized, let alone an entire team?? I mean, I'm your sister, for fuck's sake, who do they think kept you-"

"Jules!"

"What?"

"They want me to coach. Head fucking coach, little sister. And I made Kellan tell them I would only go if you came with me."

"Come with you? Why would I-"

"Jules, the team owners want their foundation to be for military families who have lost someone. And you're going to help head it up."

I almost dropped the phone, because there was no way Daisy was going anywhere with how sweetly she was sleeping in my hand. "Max," I choked on a sob. "You didn't."

"I did, baby sis. I know you wanted to give back, and now, you can."

Our dad died on a special ops mission the Corps sent him on when I was nine, leaving our mom alone to raise Max and me on her own. A hockey superstar in college, we moved closer to campus so he could help raise me. A few of the coaching staff did all they could to watch over me while Max spent hours practicing and training while our mom worked as a nurse. And were more like family than friends.

All I wanted was to give back to other families the way we were taken care of, and Max did, too, but Pens management had other foundations we spent our time with over the span of his career with the team.

"How? Why?"

"The owners have a silent partner who has an unique vision for the team they're building. And giving back is part of it. So, I told Kellan you were part of the deal."

I plopped down on the bed, and fell back, careful not to wake the sweet little furball on my chest. "But, I like it here," I protested, but it sounded weak even to my ears. "And do you even know how to coach?"

"Chase your dreams, right, Jules?" He snorted. "The junior camps and college in-house sessions caught the eye of the owners. How, I have no idea, but hell, Jules, it's more than I ever dreamed of. I'll be the youngest coach in the NHL. And we'll be able to give back to families like ours. In Dad's name."

Tears pricked at my eyes as the smile spread across my face. "I hope the Revenge knows what they're getting into. Big brother. Try not to scare off anyone like you did when we moved here, okay?"

"You can start dating when you're 35. I told you that. Not a day before."

"When I was ten, Max! And I won't have time to date in between playing with Daisy and-" My voice caught.

"I know. So," he chuckled, "is that a yes?'

I grinned into the phone. "Yes. But. I will not move in with you. Daisy and I have a thing, and we don't want boys breaking the happiness we have going. Understood?"

"Same building, okay? Because that was part of the deal, too."

I groaned. Of course, because heaven forbid Max ever let me far from his sight, I was lucky that there were no apartments in his current building. But, I think that was Amy in HR's doing. And the chocolate truffles I sent her weekly.

A girl's gotta do what a girl's gotta do when she has an overprotective brother.

"When do we leave?"

"Three days. Time for a new adventure."

My heart caught with the words our dad had always said before our world was turned upside down.

"A new adventure. And new dreams, big brother."

"The best kind, Jules."

CHAPTER TWO

KASPARI

"*K*as, it's a great offer, and there's a signing bonus."

"It's not the money, Kellan. It never was and never will be. I've played in Carolina almost my entire career. You know I like things a certain way," I huffed. But, deep down, something inside me sparked to life.

I fucking loved playing here. But, lately, things felt stagnant. And the line, my line, was changing.

Syd, my college roommate, and I played together in Nashville our rookie year.

The guy cooked better than any winner from Master Chef.

And the asshole always made sure my Lucky Charms never ran out. Call me superstitious, but, hell, most hockey players were. Lucky Charms were my thing, and I never went a day without a bowl of magical deliciousness.

Among other things, like new socks after the second period.

Then the Canes wanted me, and hell, it was an opportunity to be the 'A' line center. And get out of the shadow of the

Preds' star player. He was a great guy, but I wanted to lead a team. There, I followed. And followed well.

But in Carolina? It was my team, at least at first. But the past few years? The team had lost the drive, and I was going through the motions.

I missed playing with guys who loved the game more than the money and fame.

"The Revenge are building their organization differently, and what they're doing is right up your alley, Kas. You know I wouldn't steer you wrong."

Kellan had been my agent when Syd and I both went in the draft ten years ago, and the first time he met with us, promised he would make sure we were happy with whatever offers we accepted. Never pressured us to take an offer just for the money.

He understood our love for the game had nothing to do with the money.

I trusted his judgment implicitly.

"They want you to be the face of their foundation. For military families, Kas. Hockey camps for the kids. It's-"

"What I wanted to do here until management decided it would take away from the game," I said, sitting up straighter. Fuck, this was getting better by the minute.

A fresh start. New team. A chance to build a dynasty. And help people like my uncle, who took me and my baby brother in after our dad was killed on deployment when I was twelve. Ian barely remembered him, but mom couldn't handle raising two boys alone. Eventually, he moved in and picked up the slack when she needed to travel for work, which ended up being more often than not. And a kid playing hockey was a lot to take on when he wasn't your own. Plus, my attitude hadn't helped.

"When do I leave?"

"As soon as you get a bag together, man. Training camp is next week, brother."

I glanced around the apartment I called home for the past eight years. It still looked like it had the week I moved in. The interior designer the team had set up the place kept things modern and clean. Besides the pictures of mom, Ian, and my uncle, I hadn't changed a thing.

Just added suits to my closet and a case for my watch collection.

A guy can't only be addicted to Lucky Charms.

"Guess I'm part of the Revenge now, Kellan."

"There's just one more thing, Kas."

"I should've known there'd be something."

"The Revenge's new head coach is Maxwell Vaughn."

The room became so silent you could hear a pin drop.

"Fucking Max Vaughn from the Pens? The asshole who threw his gloves every time we played the Pens and tried to kick my ass for some stupid check that was an accident against their goalie five years ago?"

"One and the same."

"Fuck."

"At least you won't be bored."

I hung my head and rubbed my eyes as I scoffed. "I'll probably be dead or suspended for fighting my coach." Shit. The Pens and the Canes didn't play each other often, but the one time ·I accidentally knocked into their goalie, Vaughn took it as a huge slight and had a thing for me ever since. We'd avoided each other for the past few seasons, but last year we'd both spent plenty of time in the penalty box at the only game we'd played against each other.

"Never a dull moment with you, Kas. Pack your Lucky Charms. You're going to be a member of the Revenge."

CHAPTER THREE

JULES

"Shots!" Sophia's voice rang out over the music, and I fought the urge to both roll my eyes and giggle uncontrollably.

Because I was on cloud freaking nine.

Yes, my apartment wasn't ready for over two weeks when we arrived in Seattle. Yes, my office at the rink still wasn't finished. But it will be in two days. But, I started my dream job, and working with people who have just as much passion as I do about the foundation.

And since the Revenge facilities, other than the players' area, aren't complete, a slew of support staff that aren't involved directly with players have been in temporary offices. Which was how I met Sophia. And how I ended up here, dancing and buzzed.

Free from the watchful eye of Coach Maxwell. My big brother might have retired as a player, but hockey ran in his blood like ice. I loved watching the game, but my coordination on skates was a detriment to my health and others' physical well-being.

Freedom in the form of not having to live in the same

building as my big brother? Worth the wait. I renegotiated terms before agreeing to move across the country. Max stubbornly held his ground for almost a week. Nevertheless, I refused to back down. The Revenge hopefully moved my things this morning from the corporate temporary apartment. Tonight, *my* bed and pillows awaited me to slumber happily in them.

Along with Daisy and her gigantic kitty carpet palace.

My kitten deserved the best, considering Max moved us across the country with him.

As I tipped the shot my new bestie thrust into my hand only seconds before, I puckered my lips and shook my head. The alcohol burned its way down.

And the little voice in my head, empowered by my alcohol and club dancing escapade, whispered how long it had been since I got laid.

Eight months.

Longer than that if I counted good sex.

Thank God for battery operated boyfriends.

A girl had to take care of herself when her brother scared off anyone who even thought about breathing in her airspace.

Maxwell Vaughn rarely let anyone near his 24-year-old little sister. Until I moved into the building that only had one vacancy nine months ago to get away from him, and his nighttime visits whenever he thought I had company.

Big brother problems.

It still didn't help my love life much, because everyone in the Burgh knew about his semi goon-like personality on the ice. Since I was his sister, they were afraid he was going to cross-check them when he turned his steel blue gaze on them.

They didn't call him Ice Man for nothing.

And here I was, like Elsa, trapped in a castle far away from the rest of the world.

Except I wasn't making frozen fractals or missing out on the world by choice. Without Marshmallow to keep me company. Which was why I had Daisy now.

Seattle offered an opportunity to turn things around, starting tonight. Big brother had been so occupied with getting the team on the ice and reviewing everything and all things puck related. They assigned me to help set up the team's foundation with Alicia Cross, who was a barracuda at fundraising. She left me to do the outreach and planning of events. Which I loved. My team was amazing. Across town. Away from everything fun.

Until tonight. And lucky for me, vodka had a tendency to bring out the side of me that Max never knew existed.

I scanned the room as Sophia giggled next to me, wondering who I could find to help break the eight-month drought as soon as possible.

"God, it will be so damn amazing to be in the arena. And not have to drive across town in traffic!"

"Please, across town? At least you have somewhere to call home! I've been living out of a suitcase, and poor Daisy misses her catnip and grass."

She sneezed, almost spilling the vodka shot that appeared miraculously in her hand. Several of the other girls, and a few of the guys, on the 'Venge Squad, were dancing a few feet away or grabbing drinks on the bar.

The league's newest expansion team needed a promotional team of epic proportions. Or so the new owners had said when they hired Sophia to head up all things 'Vengeful. From community outreach, which was how we met, to prepping for in-game shenanigans, she organized it all. Including the hiring of social media managers, players' liaisons who helped the guys manage their accounts if they chose, and the

Ice Scrapers, who were getting TikTok famous just from the practices the team had them attend.

"Daisy is a spoiled princess, and I approve. Even if she jumped me when I picked you up this morning."

I shrugged a shoulder. "She's feisty. What can I say? She hisses at Max, so be glad you're not him."

"Playful for me, and hissy for head coach?" She sighed as she tipped back her third (or was it her fifth?) shot. "I love that pussy...cat."

With a grimace, I drank what I swore was my last, and laughed. "You've been waiting to say that, haven't you?"

"Hell. Yes. Let's go see what Seattle's finest have to offer before we really buckle down tomorrow!"

We shimmied through the crowd, and for the first time in months, I knew where I was headed. And nothing was going to stand in my way.

∿

So, it seemed something was going to stand in my way. The one guy I thought I found at the club to help me end my drought?

Tripped and ended up breaking his arm as we walked out the door.

He refused to let me go with him in the car to the hospital, but gave me his card.

Truth be told, he was nice. But the one kiss we shared didn't curl my toes. Even in the slightest.

But the entire time, the back of my neck tingled with the feeling of something I couldn't put my finger on. Not exactly Spidey-sense, but almost like there were eyes following me, especially on the dance floor.

Where I had way too much fun grinding and spinning and enjoying every single shot I took.

And then the trip happened. Maybe I was trying too hard, but that feeling of being watched spurred me on. Right until the subtle snap I heard when the poor guy whose name I never got tripped as we walked toward the exit, Sophia in tow.

So here I stand, drought still in place, putting my new key into the door of my new home for the foreseeable future.

Just me and my pussy cat.

And my Battery Operated Boyfriend.

CHAPTER FOUR

KASPARI

I rarely go out to clubs anymore. They're too loud, and filled with douchebags that think I want to fight them just because of my size and who I am.

Hell yes, I'll check you if you deserve it. Or go after my goalie. Though the D usually takes care of that.

But fuck.

Having the guy who hated me more than I hate celery as my new head coach was like being the low guy on the totem pole even though I was the captain of my team. And the best damn player they had other than Jacob Hale.

But fuck if Max Vaughn was still holding a grudge about a hit that was an accident two years ago. Our tussles, though few, made the highlight reel every damn time. Good thing I knew not to run my mouth off. I knew without a doubt, Coach was looking for a reason to either get me cut, or get me to quit.

Both options were a non-negotiable. Nobody broke me.

Practice had been brutal.

My linesmen convinced me to go out for one drink, even though I was bone ass tired and just wanted to fall face first on my bed. Hale might be defense, but he's just as fucking good as I am.

It's not cocky when you're telling the truth. And given that they got us both, I know management is serious about winning the cup sooner rather than later.

So am I.

This clubbing shit, though? I'd rather be at home, reading a book or catching up on Vikings Valhalla on Netflix. Two hours was my limit on my best day. Today, I needed a hot shower and my bed.

Until my eyes caught sight of her.

It wasn't only that she was beautiful. She was, but she radiated joy and was so sexy, my mouth was watering like Pavlov rang a bell and she was dinner.

Long, brown hair streaked with gold like a mermaid who spent hours wishing she had feet on the beach. Yep, I had a thing for Ariel when I was younger. Girl cousins who loved Disney princesses and made me watch all the movies.

And watching her dance, and seeing her smile? The way her golden brown eyes danced when she laughed?

Call me Prince Eric.

To hell with the hot shower. Now I needed an ice bath. Thank God tomorrow was a team practice later in the morning rather than the every other day 6 a.m. call time.

Season opener was in three days, and fuck, I was ready to go, despite it all.

"One more, Kas?" Hale yelled over the music, looking as tired as I was. We both wanted to prove that we were still at the top of our game.

Maybe too much.

I tipped my bottle towards him. "This is my one more."

He smirked. "Same, man."

My eyes went back to the girl who drew me in like a magnet, only to see her weaving through the crowd with

14

some douchebag who looked way too happy staring at her ass as her hips swayed in front of him.

Oh, hell no.

I nodded at Jake, and followed behind them, staying far enough behind that there was distance between us, but not so far that I lost sight of her. As they passed a group of guys, douchebag high fived one with an expression that said he knew exactly how douchey he was.

Nail in his not-getting-laid coffin.

A second later, I was right alongside them as they neared the three steps that took them up a level and just a few feet away from the exit, and there just so happened to be a chair right alongside where they were walking.

Was it my fault if the girls in front of me moved just enough so that he tripped over it while he was leering at my girl?

Not at all.

CHAPTER FIVE

JULES

The door swung open with barely a creak, but Daisy, in all her fluffy cuteness, heard the whoosh of air and barrelled towards me. She skittered to a stop, staring up at me with her big green eyes.

I scooped her up, cradling her little body as she purred away, and slipped off my heels with a sigh. "Looks like it's just us, Daisy May. And maybe Mr. Buzzworthy. If I charged him and didn't pack him under everything," I muttered, because with my luck, my battery operated longstanding date was packed away in one of the boxes I was still waiting for the moving company to bring in the morning.

The bag next to my bed sat, zipped and undisturbed. "Voila!!! Looks like they dropped off the good stuff, baby!"

After feeding Daisy, I scampered back to my room, and pulled out the purple wonder that kept me sane during the no boys situation I'd found myself embroiled in.

A girl needs to release tension, and I might just like to do it once a day. Or more.

The room felt warmer than usual for this time of year as I got ready for bed. I went to the window next to the bed and opened it just enough to feel the cool breeze on my over-heated skin. The bumps on my skin rose as I recalled how it felt when I thought someone was watching when I was dancing. How it felt, knowing that every move I made was making *him* need to watch. Every smile, laugh, and touch along my skin meant to be seen.

The need to release the pressure between my thighs intensified, and I let out a moan. I never picked up random guys, and even if I did, Max always found a way to circumvent any fun I might've had.

Which was probably for the best, really,

No sex with someone other than one of my toys was better than bad sex with someone I didn't care about. Or at least liked.

Thankfully, battery operated items had to like their owners, or they never got used. And my favorite toy, Mr. Buzzworthy, was used far more often than I cared to admit.

Stupid romance novels and their perfectly imperfect book boyfriends. And stupid vodka shots that made me wish they were more than just fiction.

A girl could dream and fantasize. Especially about tall, dark, and incredibly handsome strangers who watched them.

Hey, it's my fantasy, and I can make my swoon worthy MMC anything I want.

Ugh, hopefully not a hockey player. Because I might just have had my fill of the overbearing, puck bunny loving players to last a lifetime.

And in my fantasy, Mr. Tall, Dark, Handsome NOT a hockey player made me show him what I wish he was doing to me, using my favorite single person date night toy.

I slid my skirt up, hooking one finger around the thin strap of my thong, and pulled the thin strip of material down. I flung them with my foot, giggling and thanking my lucky stars that no one could see me in my vodka-induced horniness. Which was also kind of sad, but all of those thoughts were going to disappear in just a few moments with a flick of a switch.

My fingers skimmed up my thigh, and I propped my foot up on the small padded stool I had plopped next to the window this morning when the furniture Max bought me arrived. I let my mind wander into the fantasy of my phantom lover watching me, telling me what to do.

"That's it, beautiful. Show me how wet it makes you, knowing I'm watching you. Thinking about you. Naked and writhing beneath me. Show me how much you want to touch yourself. How much you want to come for me. How you'll get yourself off."

My fingers brushed my clit, and I gasped, so lost in my fantasy, that I didn't care about the open window. Or that anyone could walk by. But at this late hour, my fantasy was just for myself, and oh my god, was it a good feeling.

I shuddered as I worked my fingers in a circle, rubbing and panting as I neared my release.

"Oh no, beautiful girl. I want you to ride that toy. Show me what you'd do if that was my cock. Slide it into your wet pussy, and beg me to come."

I pressed the button, and the vibration against my clit made me gasp loudly in pleasure. I worked the tip inside, and slowly moved it in and out, moaning at the sensations. Losing myself in the faceless stranger I created. His orders, his eyes on me.

"I need you to come for me, beautiful. Come apart, and show me how much you wish that was me inside you, making you scream my name, over and over. Don't you dare stop. That's it, gorgeous. Come for me while I watch."

The need built in me until it exploded, and I rode the wave until I was panting, my skirt pulled up, and my inner thighs wet from coming so hard.

If only reality was as good as my fantasies…

CHAPTER SIX

KASPARI

"*H*oly shit," I murmured.

Twenty minutes after leaving the club, Hale dropped me off after we deposited Coleman Sunders on his couch, and I had just turned after waving goodbye to walk up the steps to my place when I heard it.

The fucking hottest sounds in the world.

There was a girl, somewhere within earshot, getting off. My mind spun, and I heard whoever it was gasping, and was suddenly extremely jealous of the lucky bastard who got to hear those sounds up close and personal.

But when I listened closely, the throaty feminine noises weren't followed by some dude getting off.

Holy. Shit.

I looked up to the second floor of my building, the same floor I moved into only days before, and noticed a curtain ruffle, caught in the wind, outside an open window. On my floor.

I was far enough away that I could see clearly into the apartment, yet close enough that I could hear exactly what was happening.

A window framing a female form in shadow, but with enough light that I caught the faint glimpse of her, legged up, and dress hiked up.

And using a fucking toy to get off. Transfixed, I couldn't move, let alone get out a coherent thought. Because she was getting so close to coming that my fucking dick stood up and took notice, and I lost all thought to the head who should do the thinking.

I couldn't make out her face, but there was something about her that felt vaguely familiar. Then she shifted, hair falling as her head fell back.

And though I hadn't gotten the clearest look of the girl at the club I was almost positive it was her. The way she moved, the pitch of her moans so like the throaty laugh from earlier.

Like a perverted teenager standing outside peeping in, I watched as she climaxed. Damn, she was so beautiful.

When her head fell forward, she sucked in a few breaths, then gathered herself together.

Not wanting to get caught like some perv, I quickly, and painfully, let myself into the building. When I got to my floor, I tried not to look in the direction of her door. Wondering if she was asleep. And what she was wearing.

Guess it's time for that cold shower.

"WHERE THE HELL are my Lucky Charms?'"

"Hold up, Kas, they're in the commissary with the rest of the food." Andrew, the equipment manager, said as he dropped off my gear.

"Fuck, what if someone eats them? Messing with a guy's routine on opening night is bullshit," I muttered.

"The guys all know. No worries. Promise. I'll grab the-"

I let out a frustrated growl. "No, I'll go. Fuck." The

hallway was buzzing with energy when I stepped out of the locker room. Even though the puck drop wasn't for almost three and a half hours, the staff of the Revenge were moving at an excited, frantic pace.

An entirely unfamiliar situation than I'd ever been in. I loved NC, and the Canes were my home. But here? There was a hunger and a sense of taking what we wanted. And we'd worked our asses off training.

The energy permeated every level of the organization, and fuck, was I here for it.

Longest hallway ever, I thought as I turned the corner and stalked into the commissary, looking for my damn box of magical deliciousness.

Only to stop short when I spotted it on the table.

In front of a gorgeous and fucking adorable brunette with a high pontytail, smiling with undisguised delight at her bowl. Filled with my fucking Lucky Charms.

Holy. Shit.

My jaw practically dropped to the floor before I picked it up.

Head spinning as I realized she was the same fucking girl I'd watched get off through her window last night.

Great. Peeping Tom, meet last night's fantasy.

And she was eating my damn Lucky Charms like she had never had them before.

My. Lucky. Charms.

I stood there, gawking like a teenager getting his first boner as my eyes tracked her spoon traveling from the bowl to her perfectly shaped cupid bow mouth. And when she moaned, my hard-on went from half-mast to hallelujah.

And suddenly, I didn't care that she held my pregame routine hostage with every lift of her spoon. My eyes followed it two more times before I steeled myself and tried to get a sliver of anger to reappear. She interrupted my pregame and was the reason I jacked off twice last night.

No way in hell she would hear that from my lips, though.

I stalked towards her, glaring because those were mine. And I didn't share.

You'd share with her if she let you watch her again, idiot.

Great, now the voice in my head had an opinion. And he was right.

"Those," I jabbed a finger at the box. "Are mine."

Eyes like an autumn sunset crept slowly up to meet mine, mid chew, and the breath sucked out of my lungs. They tracked from the box back to meet my eyes, and it took everything I had not to stare at the silver of skin exposed by the zipper of her Revenge official team sports hoodie. "There wasn't a name on them or anything. And I was hungry."

The fantasy of her wearing my hoodie played in my head. My hoodie, and nothing else, except a pair of knee socks.

Shit.

I narrowed my eyes and tried to snatch the box, but she swiped it before I could.

"Manners?" She rolled her eyes. "What if I want a second bowl? They *are magically delicious,* after all."

Fuck. I bet her lips were magically delicious. "Yes, but they're *mine.*" I grabbed the box and shook it. "These are in my contract."

"Ugh, I should've known. Another overbearing hockey player who thinks he can do whatever he wants," she muttered.

"Fine," I huffed. I spun around, and within seconds returned to the table with a bowl and spoon, plopping down in the chair opposite her. "But let's be clear, Cricket. If you mess up my game, the Lucky Charms are out for you, got it?"

She paused, spoon halfway to her mouth. "Wait, this is your superstition, isn't it?" Her eyes widened, hands fluttered in a shooing motion. "Get away. I do not want that kind of pressure."

"Nope. Too close to warm-ups." I sat down, poured a bowl of marshmallow happiness and splashed milk from the carton I grabbed off the table along with my spoon. "Can't mess with a guy's pregame routine, Cricket."

"Cricket? My name's-"

I held up my hand. "Less talking, more eating."

She glared at me, and the spark in their depths made me want to do more to make it appear again and again. To keep her looking at me.

And not just because I knew how sexy she sounded when she came.

It was more than that. I shifted, my happy dick not making life easy at the moment, and ate without saying another word.

Chewing spoonful after spoonful, I tried to focus on the fact that I was on the cusp of opening night of what could be the best season of my career, and not the girl sitting across from me.

CHAPTER SEVEN

JULES

"*H*oly hell, that was a *game*," Sophia squealed as she gave me a hug. Her shoulder length black hair bounced as she grinned, still in her Revenge Hype Team gear.

Somewhere in the building, most likely in the locker room, Max was celebrating his first win as an NHL coach. And while I wanted in on the party, I'd had enough of hockey players growing up. Boisterous and loud, I already knew what the locker room would be like. A girl could only take so many egos, year after year.

"It was a great opener," I agreed. I sat in the suite with our mom, who cried and shared half a pizza with me before she ran down to hug Max before she caught her flight.

"Are you going to 32?" she asked, scanning the crowd of people behind me. The hallway was a cluster of families, team members, and Revenge staff in various stages of celebration and getting things ready for the next game in two days. Her eyes widened a fraction, and I glanced over my shoulder to see what had caught her attention.

Max rambled our way, shaking hands with anyone who

extended their hand. His smile was contagious, just like it had been when he first started playing. My earliest memories were of his smile after a win, which was more often than not. But seeing him in a suit and tie instead of the sweaty uniform was still taking me time to adjust to.

"Jules, there you are! Why didn't you come down?"

I rolled my eyes as I gave him a hug. He squeezed me and lifted me off my feet before setting me back down. My big brother just grinned as I punched him in the arm playfully. "You know locker room antics are not my thing." I turned to Sophia. "Sophia, have you met my brother Max? Sophia runs the Revenge Hype Team, Max."

"Nice to meet you, Sophia," Max said before waving to someone behind us. "I have a press conference, so if you'll excuse me."

"Likewise," Sophia murmured as Max gave me one more quick hug, then rushed off toward the media room. But not before the two shared a second glance. Sophia caught me grinning at her. "What? He's cute." She shrugged one shoulder. "But, I know better than to date where I drool, if you catch my meaning. So, 32, yes? That's where the higher-ups reserved space for the season opener celebratory shenanigans. Just a few minutes."

"The moving company was supposed to deliver the rest of my things today, and I haven't been home yet. Plus, Daisy is all alone," I hedged.

"Jules. Come on, fifteen minutes. Your brother won his NHL coaching debut. I get not wanting to be enveloped in the chaos, but…"

I groaned. She was right. And fifteen minutes wouldn't matter in the grand scheme of things. "Fine, but if Daisy gets an abandonment complex, you're paying for kitty therapy."

"If your pussy needs therapy, I'll gladly help out," she snickered with a laugh.

"Ugh, don't remind me," I groaned. "After that poor guy broke his arm, maybe I should just stick to battery operated trysts alongside a hot romance novel."

She looped her arm through mine as we headed down the hall, weaving through the crowd. "Don't give up hope. There's always a chance encounter with a stranger or hottie possible at any time. Always. Maybe even tonight."

"I just want my bed, Soph. And my kitty."

THREE HOURS LATER, I was trudging up the stairs, thankful that tomorrow was Saturday, and I had nothing to do except have dinner with Max at his place later in the evening. Hopefully, the movers delivered the rest of my stuff so I could spend the day unpacking.

As I neared my door, I could hear Daisy mewing, which was unusual and made me quicken my pace. The hallway outside my door was wet. Not flooded, but enough so that I slipped and had to grab the knob to my apartment.

There were other team members living in the building, and the renovated building was modern, sleek, and I actually loved my place more than my one in Pittsburgh. I slid the key in the lock and turned the door.

To find my apartment was the source of the leaking water flowing into the hall. And poor Daisy perched on the cupboard above the counter in the kitchen area. "Oh, baby, come here!"

She mewed again, and when I neared, reached her little paws down as I gathered her against my chest, her little body shivering. I looked up and saw the source of the water dripping from the ceiling into the living room and near the door to my bedroom.

"Oh no," I moaned, and ran into the bedroom, only to see

everything drenched from the leak emanating from above. The only thing that survived of the things I brought with me was the bag I packed, which I left by the door this morning before I left for the day.

As I turned away from the wet mess, I noticed none of my other boxes were anywhere in sight.

Most of my belongings were missing, but that may be a blessing in disguise. At least some of my things weren't drenched. I cuddled Daisy and dialed the property management company. I yanked open the door, and rushed into the hallway.

Only to slam into Mr. Lucky Charms himself as the line rang until going to voicemail.

"Woah, there, Cricket. Where's the fire?"

Daisy snuggled into my hair, and I hissed at him, "There's no fire, it's a flood, and my entire apartment is wet." He caught me as I tried to balance and almost burst into tears. "And none of my things are here except for random sheets and stuff, which is good, but the only clothes I have are in my bag, and even then, I don't have any of my stuff and poor Daisy is terrified."

"Okay, Cricket, come on. Let's get you both somewhere dry, then call the property manager. Do you have your bag?"

I thrust my phone at him. "It went to voicemail."

He popped his head into my apartment, and let out a low whistle. "I see a Revenge team bag. Is that it?"

I nodded, sniffling. Daisy mewed as she snuggled deeper into my hair. My purse still sat on my shoulder, thankfully.

"Ok, come on, let's go to my place. I'm two doors down."

"Are you still mad about the Lucky Charms?" I asked as I followed him.

He snorted. "No way. I played my best game tonight. So now you're stuck with me. And my Lucky Charms." The door swung open, and he gestured for me to go inside. "I'll call Mark. He had to fix my sliding door the other night, so I have his home number. Bathroom is through there." He eyed Daisy. "Does *it* need a litter box?"

Again, my head bobbed.

"Ok, I'm going to see if I can grab it from your place and call Mark." He paused, and added, "I'm Kas, by the way."

"I know, I watched the game. Nice goals, by the way."

He smirked. "Told you, Cricket, you're my new Lucky Charm."

CHAPTER EIGHT

KASPARI

Great, now the girl I stroked one off to was in my damn apartment.

With the biggest damn eyes and pouty lips and just about the best curves I'd ever seen. Or had pressed against me for three seconds. When she adorably stumbled into my arms.

With a cat.

I hate cats. Even small little balls of fur because they grow up to be cats. And all cats are assholes.

"Hey, Mark! Yeah, it's Kas. No, everything at my place is great. But there's a leak in the floor above, and the apartment below is kinda having its own mini river take over. Looks like it's stopped," I said as I craned my neck at the ceiling. "But the damage is only in her apartment."

What he said next stopped me dead in my tracks. "No fucking way." With a heavy sigh, I dropped my head, cursing my luck. Squishy noises echoed in the empty apartment as I made my way to the bathroom, grabbing the dry litter box and scooping up the box next to it that held a few cans of kitten food and little cellophane balls. Also dry, thankfully.

"No, she can stay in my spare room for now. No sense in trying to find anything tonight. I'll tell her. Thanks, Mark."

I hit end and cursed my luck once more.

The hot girl in my apartment that I had fantasies about last night?

My coach's little sister.

The guy who had it in for me, and would no doubt make my life miserable if he found out.

With a grunt, I opened the door to the hallway with my foot, and sat down the demon animal's things, and went back in, heading to the bathroom where I found one of those fancy pink vinyl bags filled with product. Knowing how much my sister loved her beauty products, I grabbed that and the short fluffy robe hanging on the back of the door. And did my best not to imagine her tempting body, all curves, wrapped tight in the terry cloth. Legs showing, and tie begging to be undone as she slid her hand up-

Concentrate, asshole, and not on how hot she sounded through her window last night.

Doing my best to stuff it all in my arms, I headed down the hall and nudged the door open with one foot, then kicked it closed once I was inside. A little furball of unholiness ran towards me, meowing like it was telling me to go to hell.

"Listen here, demon spawn, no getting comfortable, you hear? Temporary lodgings." I whispered as I ignored the fact the little thing was kinda cute.

Nope. Not falling for it. Cats are evil. Even if they're as adorable as their owner. I set the box of cat supplies on the kitchen island and took the rest of what I grabbed for her to the bathroom.

"I grabbed a few things-"

I stopped mid-sentence.

Running water and soft moans caught my attention, and my eyes shot from the little demon fluff ball at my feet to the

30

slightly ajar bathroom door. My feet moved forward of their own volition, searching for the same voice that had me transfixed the night before.

And my dick took notice, too, coming to half-mast.

Well, fuck.

The kitten skittered towards the couch, leaping up and curling into a tight ball. I glared at it, refusing to let the thought of how cute it looked invade my mind.

Mostly due to the soft and incredibly sexy sounds coming from the bathroom just a few feet away. Through the slit of the doorway, I could barely make out her image in the fogged up mirror, her sweet body under the spray of the massage showerhead I insisted on having in both bathrooms of my apartment.

Damn thing was amazing after a grueling practice or game that went into OT.

And evidently, my Cricket thought it was pretty awesome too, judging from the noises she made and the way her head was thrown back.

Fuck, I wished I could see her expression right now. After hearing and seeing her last night, my mind filled with images of her lips parted, eyes desperate as she trembled when her body orgasmed.

Not just through a window, or through the steamy open door to my bathroom. I wanted to watch her fall apart in front of me. To watch what made her quiver, gasp, and lose control.

Then I wanted to do all of that to her, and more. All night.

Shit.

The door swung open, stopping me in mid-fantasy as my temporary roommate stood in the smallest towel I owned wrapped haphazardly around her naked, dripping body. Leaving nothing to my very active imagination.

"Oh! Sorry, I just needed a shower. I cry in the shower

sometimes and it just makes everything better. Should I have not?"

"No, it's fine." And just like that, half-mast stepped it up a notch. The flush of her skin, the glow she wore like a damn gold winning medal, reminding me of her shower activities. Her fucking lips pouted, and I thrust her things at her, before brushing past and setting the litter box on the floor.

And the little demon ran past us both, sniffed it and jumped in. "At least he's litter box trained."

She wrinkled her nose. Distracting me. "She's trained. Daisy is the best kitten ever. And a girl."

"Got it," I said, not missing the way her chest rose and fell with each breath, barely contained by the towel. We stared at each other for a few seconds before I croaked out, "I grabbed some of your things, Cricket. Since you can't exactly sleep in your place, at least for tonight."

Her hand adjusted the towel, but it still hid nothing. I began to think she was doing it on purpose as her teeth scraped along her bottom lip. "Why do you keep calling me that?"

"What?" I barely heard her words, stuck on wondering if she tasted as sweet as she sounded when she came.

"Cricket."

Giving my head a mental shake, I canted my head and studied her before I answered. More to calm my eager dick down than anything else. "Some cultures consider a cricket either good or bad luck when I first called you that. Call it a hunch that day.. Because now I played my best game in years, you're my new Lucky Charm." I smirked, loving how her eyes widened. "So be prepared to have *Lucky Charms* with me for the foreseeable future, Cricket."

I loved the fire in her eyes and decided right then and there, I would not tell her I knew who she was. There was no way I would let Maxwell Vaughn get in between me and my new lucky charm.

Especially if she let me watch her get off a third time. And by the way her pupils were dilating, I'd bet my next three starting spots she was as turned on as I was right now.

Jules Vaughn might be the little sister of my coach and rival, but, damn, I wanted to make her mine.

Face flush, she suddenly looked back at the bathroom door, and down at the floor, as if realizing where I stood. And what I might've seen.

"Did you like what you saw, Kaspari?"

CHAPTER NINE

JULES

I moistened my lips, because now that I finally could breathe after the trauma of seeing my things soaked (well, not all of them), my body decided to take notice of the man in front of me. All six feet plus of him.

Every defined and bulging muscle. The eyes. The perfect amount of scruff on his face, neatly trimmed, somehow made his lips even more sensual than they would have been without the sexy facial hair.

Did I mention the eyes? Framed by thick lashes, and sparkling with humor and heat, locked with mine, they were pools I wanted to dive into and drown in for hours.

Dear lord, I needed to get laid.

Badly.

When it dawned on me I had left the door to the bathroom open while I showered and relieved a bit of stress from the day, I didn't stop. Especially when I noticed my hot hockey player knight in shining armor watching. The guy I knew I should stay away from had the perfect view of all my…activities.

"Did you like what you saw, Kaspari?"

I licked my lips again, fascinated by the way his eyes tracked the movement. Pupils dilated.

"MEEEWWWW."

We jumped apart, and he smacked into the door, causing it to slam into the wall, scaring Daisy as she skittered away. I giggled, and took my fluffy pink robe from him, slipping my arms into the sleeves and loosely tying it before letting the towel drop out from underneath. His eyes darted to the front, where the lapels were barely covering my breasts.

"Sorry, Daisy gets moody when she's hungry." He handed me the rest of my things, and my mouth opened in surprise. He grabbed all my beauty products from the counter in the bathroom. Which meant he had to have gone back in at least twice into the swampy mess that was my new apartment. "You brought my things?"

He grunted, and ran a hand through his hair, like he just realized how much effort he dished out for some girl and her kitten. A shoulder lifted and fell, despite that, my eyes were glued to him. "Why wouldn't I, Cricket?"

He asked the question like it was silly of me to even consider he wouldn't have rushed back into the Niagara Falls that was happening in my place.

Okay, so maybe that was an exaggeration.

But the way he said and did all kinds of tingly things to parts of me we longing for those long fingers to touch me. My breath quickened, and suddenly, I was very aware of exactly how naked I was beneath my fluffy robe.

My loosely tied, fluffy robe.

Daisy mewed again, and I spun before I made a complete fool and begged him to do all the things the look in his eyes promised.

A hand shot out, handing me a small can of kitten food. I glanced over my shoulder with a quizzical look.

"Here. For...Daisy?"

I nodded, unable to form a decent sentence without saying *I want you, Kaspari. And I love the idea of you watching me.*

Actually, those were more words than I was capable of, so I settled for grabbing the can and focusing on feeding my little gray bestie.

I bent over, fully aware of how the back of my robe rode up along the back of my thighs. And careful not to show more than I should. When I straightened, his breath heated the skin where my neck and collarbone met.

"And hell yes, Cricket, I liked what I saw."

How the hell could I resist that?

Slowly.

Because I didn't trust myself to not throw myself at him.

This is what happens when your big brother has been overprotective of you since you were nine years old. And scared off every single boyfriend or potential hookup you've tried to have except for three guys. Two of which he set you up with because of 'the talk' beforehand for the date he planned for us. And those were the only guys who made it to my door most of the time.

"And what exactly did you see?"

He closed the short distance between and gave me enough time before he answered to move away if I chose.

I held my ground and refused to look away.

"Oh, Cricket. You're beautiful. Seeing the way you lose yourself?" He leaned in, brushing his nose along mine. "Sexiest thing I've ever fucking seen. Knowing you were touching yourself. Making yourself cum?"

I shivered as molten heat went straight to my pussy just with that simple touch. "Mhmm?"

Kaspari smirked and moved as he whispered in my ear. "Cricket, if I could watch you do that after every game, I'd make damn sure we won. Every time."

"Is that all it takes?" I asked breathlessly.

"As long as you eat Lucky Charms before each game, I'm always going to try. But, if I get to see you touch yourself, and hear the way you sound? Fuck, Cricket. Hell. Yes."

My eyes fluttered closed as his scent enveloped me. Woodsy combined with a clean scent that reminded me of soap. The kind you wanted to use, so you smelled like the really good boy smell.

Masculine. Subtle. Intoxicating.

When I opened them, his face was close enough to touch, his breath mingling with mine.

Breathing the same air. Heat radiated between us.

I wanted to burn, to get lost in his touch. His fire.

He might skate on ice, but here and now, he made my body burn with a fire I needed stoked.

I admitted it to myself that, yes, I may have let the door open, not just so Daisy wouldn't be scared. But because I wanted him to see me.

Sitting across from him before the game, I had to clench my thighs together and stop my mind from having crazy fantasies as his eyes studied me with such intensity.

Hockey players were off-limits. Not just because my brother was the head coach of the Revenge. But because I grew up around them and saw how they fell in with puck bunnies. Or had egos that I just didn't want to deal with.

Or deal with my brother.

But Kaspari?

I wanted, even just for tonight, to get lost in his eyes. The way he looked at me.

Like I was a dessert he wanted to lick the plate clean even after he ate the very last crumb.

"Kas?"

"Cricket?"

I bit my lip, my hand going to the belt lightly tied at my

waist. "I think winning the home opener deserves a special celebration. Don't you?"

The way his head jerked as he dropped his gaze to where I slowly undid the belt, letting the sides slowly fall open. "Cricket, there's nothing more that I want than to commemorate tonight than making you scream my name as you cum. But, I don't want to take advantage of you."

I let out a frustrated huff of air and dropped the robe to the ground, squaring my shoulders. "Who says I'm not taking advantage of you, hotshot?"

He growled, taking in my naked form. "Fuck, baby."

I let a hand run up his chest, fingering the buttons of his dark blue dress shirt, undoing them as I made my way up to his thick neck. Why was he so damn sexy? I hated hockey players. Growing up with them made me immune to their charms.

Maybe that was it. He wasn't trying to charm me or get into my pants.

I was the one standing in front of him, naked, and trying to undress him. All the while, dark desire burned in his eyes.

My hands trembled, working the buttons as he watched through hooded eyes. I knew he wanted me as much as I wanted him.

He reached up, stilling my hands. "If we do this, Cricket, understand I'm not a one and done kinda guy. Tonight. Or later."

My knees wobbled, because I wasn't sure if he meant orgasms, sex, or…making this a part of his routine.

Depending on how well he carried out his promise to make me scream, my drought would end in spectacular fashion.

I was so here for it.

CHAPTER TEN

KASPARI

*H*er eyes bore into mine.

"I hope you're a man of your word, because I haven't screamed anyone's name in a really long time."

"Oh, Cricket, I never back down from a challenge."

Her eyes lit with the same fire from when she tried to keep my Lucky Charms from me. And fuck, it turned me on.

"Oh, so I'm a challenge?"

I snaked my arm around her waist, pulling her naked curves flush against me. "Never. You're more than that. You're mine."

A soft gasp escaped from her as I claimed her mouth, unable to hold myself back any longer. I took full advantage of the moment, slipping my tongue along her lips as she opened for me. Tasting her. Taking her.

Claiming her for my own.

The sister of the man who wanted to make my life hell.

But I didn't care. She was my lucky charm. The girl who made everything fall into place. And I wanted her.

Now.

"Oh my God," she gasped as I slid my hands down to her hips, and lifted her, palming her round ass in both of my hands. Her legs wrapped around my waist, and I felt her heat against my stomach and groaned into her mouth. I took and took, stealing her breaths and whimpers.

I turned, angling towards the couch in the center of the room. Thankful for once that I let my sister talk me into buying the fucking monstrosity. It was huge, oversized and had a plush ottoman that fit the length of the couch itself.

Perfect to take advantage of my Cricket on. Any way I wanted.

I laid her on the cushions, pausing to finish unbuttoning my shirt, tearing it off before I reached for the button and zipper of the black trousers I wore. Her eyes followed my actions, and when she licked her lips as I reached for my zipper, my dick went all in.

"You enjoy watching me, too, Cricket?"

"Why is watching you unzip your pants such a turn on?" she moaned, writhing her luscious body and almost making me shoot my load just seeing every inch of her skin glistening either from her shower or the desire blooming between us. When her hand slid down to the apex of her thighs, I bit back my groan. Fingers touching the slit I couldn't wait to run my tongue along. Circling her clit as her hips bucked, begging for attention.

"Because you know I'm going to fuck you soon. And you love when I watch you, knowing my dick is going to take that pussy hard and make you scream, over and over. All night." I deliberately drew out lowering my zipper as her fingers continued to slide along her heat. "Spread yourself for me, baby. Let me see you. All of you."

She obeyed me, eyes fluttering and back arching. God, she was a damn dream. All curves and temptation. Fingers spread her lips, and I growled at the sight.

She was perfect. Glistening, swollen, and so beautiful. Her skin flushed. Lips parted, panting. Breasts full and begging for my mouth.

"Show me how you make yourself cum, Cricket. Don't hold back."

I slipped my dick out of my boxer briefs, fisting myself as I watched the fantasy I played over in my head while she was in the shower play out in technicolor detail. Her head thrown back as she circled her clit with her fingers, using the wetness from her core. Knees spread like she knew I needed to see her like this.

She was a drug, and fuck, was I addicted.

I stroked my dick, and her eyes watched hungrily. "Do you like it when I watch you get off?"

My Cricket nodded wordlessly, both lost and found in the moment. Her movements became more frantic with each passing second. Breasts heaving, tempting me. I reached down and pulled on one nipple, just enough to elicit a gasp from her.

"Don't stop. Fuck yourself with your fingers. Show me just how you like to cum, baby." Her orgasm was building, and my dick loved seeing how close she was. That she was doing this not just for her pleasure, but for mine. I tightened my fist, imagining how tight she would be. Her sweet heat taking my dick, inner walls clenching and needing me to fuck her.

Her breaths were coming faster and faster as she worked a finger in her pussy. "Kas," she begged.

"Add another. After you make yourself cum, I'm going to fuck you, baby. I want that pussy ready for me to take you any way I want."

Her eyes darted to my fist, working my dick hard, the red tip angry and greedy. Fuck, I needed her. And I knew she saw how big I was. "Do. It. Now." I'd be damned if I would hurt

41

her, but I knew the more she played with herself, the faster I would be inside her sweet pussy. Another finger slid in and her eyes widened as I continued to fist my dick, harder and harder as she pushed herself towards her climax.

Spread open for me like the greatest gift I had ever been given. Sexy and so turned on that I let out a curse, fighting my orgasm.

"That's it, baby. Fuck your fingers until you come while I watch you," I demanded. "Such a good girl, Cricket."

Her eyes rolled back as she hit the crest of her orgasm, gasping and bucking her hips, fingers furiously taking and giving what she wanted. Head thrashing with wild abandon.

She was a masterpiece, and even more exquisite than I imagined. Seeing her through a window or steamy mirror was nothing compared to the reality.

Fuck, I wanted more.

Seconds passed as I watched her ride out her orgasm, flushed and a sheen of sweat coating her skin. Daring me to lick every delectable inch. Tasting her.

I reached down, setting my cock free, and took her fingers. Gaze locked with her as I brought them to my mouth. Sucked them clean with a satisfied growl. "Fuck, you taste better than I imagined. I need more."

I knelt between her legs, and buried my nose in her. Loving the wetness coating her, dripping and glorious. A soft gasp escaped her as I used my thumbs to spread her open, running my tongue along the most sensitive parts of her. I rubbed my nose against her clit, loving the noises she made.

She was more than addictive.

She was what I had been missing all along.

Grinning like the devil, I licked and sucked hungrily until her thighs clenched around my head, holding me in place, she demanded that I give her all the things she needed.

Suddenly, Jules opened her legs and begged, "Please, Kas, fuck me. I need you inside me."

But I wasn't done, and bit her clit just enough to make her let out a soft yelp. "Don't tell me what to do, Cricket. I told you you were going to scream my name. And I'm not stopping until you do. Multiple times, baby."

CHAPTER ELEVEN

JULES

The man had a magical tongue that had me writhing, and his words had me whimpering. And god, the things he was doing to my clit! Teasing. Teeth nipping.

My hips bucked of their own volition, and he held my thighs in place as he fucked me with his tongue. Licking. Biting. Sucking. Delirious with pleasure, legs shaking, and riding the waves of an orgasm so strong it was like an out-of-body experience.. I never wanted him to stop, but I also felt like if he did, I would never be the same.

When he pulled back, a lazy, sexy, satisfied smirk on his face, taking in every part of me on display before him, my body lit aflame.

God, I wanted him inside me as much as I wanted to stay locked down by his stare.

His eyes owned me, the desire and pure maleness across his face as he bit his lower lip, my undoing.

One finger slid along my slit, gathering the wetness there. "Tell me, Cricket. Do you like when I watch you touch yourself? When you're on display for me?"

A smirk on his face as he slid a thick finger inside me, making me moan and arch into his palm. He knew exactly how to play me. And make me want to beg for more. The sensations overwhelmed me, and I could only nod in my post orgasmic haze.

"Tell me. I need to hear you say it. Just for me."

My breath hitched as he added another, curling them, and playing me with his talented fingers. "Yes," I said, my eyes locked on his face as he glanced down to where he worked and fucked me. Spreading my pussy, his other hand on the inside of my thigh, opening me even more. "I like how you watch me."

He paused, then withdrew his fingers before he asked, "How much, Cricket?"

Hand still gripping my thigh, trapped before him, I licked my lips. "I like it. So. Much."

Slowly, he brought his fingers to my mouth. "I think you're not as innocent as you look, baby. I think you should taste how sweet you are. How fucking good this pussy tastes when you cum."

Holy. Hell. My mouth opened as his fingers traced my lips, and my tongue darted out. Tasting and loving the way he caught every second. Like I was beautiful and sexy and everything in the world to him.

Intoxicated by the way he made me come apart so easily, and how much I loved the look in his eyes. I writhed on the couch, the plush material against my bare back and his hard body before me too much.

"Kaspari, please fuck me."

His head tilted to the side, and he leaned over me, licking the wetness he coated my lips with only seconds before.

"You are stunning when you fall apart". One part of me wanted to hide away, unable to handle how he saw me, took me in, and destroyed me in the best possible way. But the other part reveled in the way he looked at me, the pleasure he took because he enjoyed watching me. My eyes narrowed, because even though I secretly liked it, I wasn't letting him off the hook that fast. He noticed my reaction and pinned me with his eyes.

"Tell me again, Cricket."

"Please. I need-" My head fell back against the cushions as he teased me, sliding his talented fingers just outside where I so desperately wanted him.

He smirked, knowing what I wanted, when I tried to get him to touch me again.

"Fuck, you don't know the half of it." The growl he let out shot straight to my pussy. "You're sexy as fuck, Jules. Making you cum is the hottest thing I've ever seen. Damn, Cricket." My breath caught as he leaned down, our breath mingling and dancing. I nearly came out of my skin when he whispered against my lips before claiming them. "My favorite Lucky Charm."

We kissed like our souls were on fire. Maybe they were. I tasted myself on his tongue as it delved into my mouth, tangling and making me moan and squirm. He kissed like he was a man starved, and my lips were the one thing he needed more than anything.

Until I felt his cock teasing my entrance, thick and hard and everything I needed.

Then I knew that after this moment, I would be ruined.

"Fuck." Kas dropped his head, foreheads touching.

A thin sheen of sweat coating our bodies.

Alarms went off in my head. "What? Is it Daisy?"

He chuckled. "No, your little demon spawn is nowhere to be seen."

"Then what?"

"I might have to watch you and do this after every win."

The smirk on his face as his fiery gaze traveled the length of my body was carnal and possessive.

God, I loved it.

He bit out a curse as he lined himself up, slowly sliding into me, and finally giving me what I begged for.

"This pussy? It's mine now, Cricket." Sweat dripping, he thrust his cock deeper with each movement, and the size of him stretched me in the most delicious ways.

"Please," I pleaded.

"Tell me, Cricket."

"Fuck me harder, Kas."

And God love the man, he lost himself in me, in the feel of our bodies joining, over and over. Using me hard, just as I begged.

Grunting and filling me, Kaspari Holken fucked me like he knew exactly what my body needed before I did. And, when he reached between our bodies, fingers circling my clit with one hand, and using the other to throw my leg over his shoulder, I screamed in pleasure. His cock hit me in the spot that made me see stars as his thumb worked magic on my clit.

I came apart in his arms, and with two more hard thrusts, he roared as he orgasmed, pushing me into the couch and knocking pillows onto the floor. The weight of his body, and the scent of his skin, were as intoxicating as the way he drew out two of the best orgasms I'd ever had.

Or was it three? I giggled.

Kas lifted himself, easing his weight off my blissed out body. "What's so funny, Cricket?"

"Just wondering if that was your second hat trick of the night."

He nuzzled my neck before nipping at the spot between my neck and collarbone. "Oh, baby, I am definitely scoring

47

on you. Again and again. And I'll take all the pussy you want to give me to celebrate."

"Meeeewwwww."

"Not funny, demon spawn."

I snorted blissfully and sighed. "You asked for it."

CHAPTER TWELVE

KASPARI

"*Y*our place is going to be a no-go zone for at least a few days." I sat my phone back down on the nightstand as Jules buried herself further into my side and mumbled incoherently.

After making sure we didn't break the couch, I scooped her up, and we took the hottest shower of my life. In more ways than one, and before she could try to get away and sleep on the couch, I dried her delicious curves off. Taking in every detail. From the firm breasts with nipples that begged to be sucked and bitten, to her round ass that I left teeth marks on, to the dandelion fuzz tattoo on her arm.

Damned if I didn't fuck her against the bathroom counter from behind while she watched our bodies taking and giving with the sexiest expression on her face before getting on her knees in front of me while I finished in her mouth.

I was done.

Then, I gave her my team hoodie, even though covering her body was the last thing I wanted to do.

Right then and there, I knew she was more than just my Lucky Charm for one night.

There's something primal about seeing a girl you just made cum multiple times, blissed out and orgasm drunk in your clothes that made you want to beat your chest and claim her for your own.

But her laugh? Shit.

When Daisy jumped up on my chest, nuzzling my face, Jules giggled at my expression and fuck if my dick didn't take immediate notice.

"I'll make up the guest room," I hedged, "if you want."

She lifted her head. "And give up the warmth of this body and all the orgasms?" Then her eyes widened. "Unless you don't want-"

I stopped her next words with my lips, threading my fingers through her hair. And kissed her full lips until she melted against me again. "I want. Fuck, do I want."

She giggled, and of course, the damn kitten chose that moment to jump on the bed.

"Cock blocker," I muttered under my breath as she purred away before snuggling up between us.

"Aw, Daisy," she crooned. "Do you like snuggling Kas as much as I do?"

The demon spawn mewed, and I knew I was in trouble.

"I can't stay here forever, but damn, the orgasms make me want to," she mused. Then her eyes turned back to me, serious and full of concern. "But, I have to tell you. My brother is really overprotective, and the minute he hears about this-"

I put my finger on her lips. "Max isn't going to say anything unless you want him to."

Her brow furrowed. "You don't know my brother." Biting her lip, she continued. "He's kinda over-the-top. Our dad died in the Corps when I was nine, and Max kind of took the big brother thing to a whole other level."

Shit. I swept a strand of hair off her face. "I get it. My dad

50

passed away in a training accident when I was younger. Which is why the Revenge's charitable foundation added to the idea of being traded."

Her eyes widened. "And it's why I moved here from Pittsburgh. That's where I work."

I knew this girl, in all her clumsy and silly, sexy glory was put in my path for a reason.

My dick agreed. "Stay as long as you need. And I'll give you a hat trick every fucking night. Or in the morning."

SWEAT DRIPPED DOWN MY FACE, but I didn't feel a thing.

Jules and Daisy, the little spawn of Satan, were still crashing in my apartment while Mark had everything fixed at her place.

Three days and countless orgasms later, I was hooked.

And it was game night. Coach ran practice like a man on a mission, and though it still felt like he had it in for me, I didn't blame him one bit.

We were all on a mission.

The Cup. Nothing less would do.

"Holken!" Max Vaughn barked at me. "Get your head on the ice, or I'll pull your start."

Asshole. I can't fucking believe Jules is related to this jackass.

I shot him a glare and skated over to my line. As I passed him, Hale muttered, "Who the fuck shit in his Cheerios."

Even if I agreed with him, I wasn't going to risk my damn spot or my lines'. Chemistry was off the hook, and considering we only played preseason together, we were miles ahead of where I thought we'd be at this point.

"Fuck this shit," Coleman Sunders, my right wing, muttered. "What the hell crawled up his ass and died?"

Marc LeCavalier skated over, flipping his stick in a spray

of ice as he stopped. "Dude's a bear over his little sister. Fucking hot, from what I hear. She stays out of the flood-light, but he got her a position with the team's foundation. And her apartment flooded, but she refused to move in with him."

"How the fuck do you know all that? What, are you the new tea spiller?" Sunders quipped.

He shrugged. "Coach was barking in his phone at her. I listen. And know things."

"Don't fucking say that shit." I glared at him.

"What?"

"That hot shit. She's not some puck bunny."

His eyebrows shot up. "Sorry, man."

"Quit the chirping," Coach yelled, blowing his whistle as he skated over to the boards. "Run the plays, not your mouths."

"Shit, if he's this crabby, I can only imagine what the hell is going to happen when he finds out Holken lives on the same floor as her."

Cole's eyebrow shot up. "Shit, you're screwed. First roughing his goalie, and then living on the same floor?" He shook his head. "I wouldn't want to be you."

JULES LEFT by the time I slunk in the door from practice, leaving me alone with Daisy, who kept trying to butter me up. But I wasn't fooled. Purring and blinking her eyes might fool some people, but not me.

"I still don't trust you, fuzzball. I'm keeping an eye on you."

She blinked up at me and hopped up on the couch. Presumably to get a better view before she turned from adorable kitten to asshole demon spawn.

I was slightly disappointed when she reached her paw towards me and mewed.

"I know, lunch time. Didn't Jules feed you before she left?"

I scooped her up and took her into the kitchen with me, football style. And the little engine that could roared to life.

"Stop brown nosing. I'm only feeding you to stay on Jules' good side. And not because you're cute. Or because I like you. Got it?" I held her out in front of me, studying her while she stared back, then set her on the floor while I grabbed the can of food from the counter.

Right next to Jules' handwritten note.

"Daisy hasn't eaten since breakfast, and Sophia is picking me up for the foundation's first family night pre-skate. I know you'll take good care of her.

See you for our Lucky Charms, big guy. And maybe I'll let you watch me later. But only if you have a good game ;)"

Damn, the woman was under my skin. Gorgeous, funny, a little clumsy, and sassy as fuck. Even if she liked kittens.

Who turned into cats.

"HEY, CRICKET," I said, sitting down at the table across from Jules. She passed the box of Lucky Charms slowly, teasing me, taunting. Licking her spoon like she knew exactly what watching her tongue work its magic did to my dick.

"Hey, Kaspari." Eyes twinkling, I suppressed a groan as she spooned another mouthful, drawing out the bite, and giving the damn spoon way too much attention.

Attention my dick was demanding. Now.

"Does this count as watching you?" I asked in a low voice. Her cheeks flushed, and her eyes darted around the room.

"Do you want it to?"

"Fuck no." I hid a grin behind a spoonful of my traditional pre-game snack. "But I do like to watch you, Cricket."

She sat up straighter, and grinned, a sultry, adorable vixen who didn't even begin to see what she did to me. "I suggest you focus on the game, and I'll really show you how you can watch me."

The noise level in the room increased as more of the guys trickled into the room. Hale stole a glance and grinned. I flipped him off when Jules wasn't paying attention.

But none of the guys said a word, because you don't mess with a guy's routine.

Or his superstitions.

Or his girl.

And make no mistake, Jules Vaughn was mine.

I just had to make her see, and survive having her brother as my coach.

No big.

And make sure her kitten didn't totally turn into an asshole.

Package deal, my Cricket and her kitten. And I intended on keeping every single part of her all to myself.

Far away from her way overprotective brother who could make my life a living hell if he found out. Both off and on the ice.

Yep. Jules and I needed to have a talk. Sooner rather than later. Especially when we played the Pens in just a few weeks. Preferably before she found out her brother had it in for me.

Hard core.

"I can't believe it took me this long to try Lucky Charms," she said over a mouthful of rainbow and unicorn marshmallows.

"I can't believe I get to watch you try them over and over for the foreseeable future," I teased gruffly, glancing around the room. But no one was paying us any attention.

She tilted her head. "My brother played hockey for as long as I can remember. And there were some crazy things the guys did to keep their superstitions going."

I pretended to be offended and shook my head before shoveling a spoonful into my mouth. My spoon waved in her direction as I swallowed. "Listen, don't knock it. I've seen streaks end because a guy forgot to turn his socks inside out, or not hit the posts in the right order."

She rolled her eyes. "And this is why I stay far away from the locker room and hockey players. I've never seen a bunch of grown men who were more afraid of forgetting a," her fingers did the quote motion, which made her cleavage show in between the lowered zipper of her hoodie, "smelly pair of socks, or their lucky roll of purple tape."

The smirk was involuntary, and I loved the way she squirmed under my gaze, and all too soon, I had to go suit up and get ready for the game. I stood, and cleared our table, then as I passed her she said, "Just remember what the rest of your…thing is, big guy."

"Oh, Cricket, I could never forget my Lucky Charm."

CHAPTER THIRTEEN

JULES

"Wait, you're what?"

"Soph, you can't say a word." My hands gripped her forearm as she stepped over the piles of towels the equipment manager dumped into the back hallway leading to the upper area of the arena where Sophia spent the entire game. "I'm serious. If Max finds out-"

"That you're shacking up with his mortal enemy?"

Stopped so abruptly, Sophia hurtled back into me. "Mortal what?"

Her mouth dropped open. "How do you not know this?"

"I'd know if you'd tell me!"

"You don't know that your brother and Holken are one of the league's biggest rivals? It's a huge story that he's even on the team, Jules." She fished her phone out of her back pocket. Fingers flying fast and furious, she added, "Like, they had one of the craziest throwdowns I've ever seen last year."

My face went to the screen of her phone as she thrust it at me. Suddenly, the hall spun around me, and I held out a hand searching for something to steady my world. When my eyes could focus again, I whispered loudly, because my chill disappeared on me, "Soph, you can't say a word."

She scoffed. "Who would I tell? Maureen? She's twenty and can barely utter a word when she has to. Jeremy is too busy trying to hit on all the fans. And I mean, *all* the fans. Your secret is safe with me." Her eyes widened. "You dirty little coach's sister! You've done the center score play on me, haven't you?"

"What?"

"You slept with him!" she whisper yelled.

This time, my chill had definitely left the building, and I grabbed her by the arm as she cackled as I dragged her into the offshoot hallway that led to the locker rooms. "I'm serious. You can't say a word. *Promise me.* Max wasn't just the best defensemen for the Pens blocking pucks. He cock blocked me nonstop."

Sophia waved at someone behind me. "Then it's my mission to make sure that my girl continues to get all the cock she wants, isn't it?"

"Oh my God, Sophia!"

Grinning bigger than the Cheshire Cat, she looped her arm through mine, flipping her hair over her shoulder as we made our way to suites to watch the game. "No one puts my girl in a corner."

"Gee, thanks, Johnny."

"Anytime, Baby. Now, let's go watch that hot side piece of yours earn that pussy tonight."

$\sim$

FOUR HOURS LATER, the steam from the shower filled the bathroom as I finished washing my hair. Citrus and pine filled the air.

Yes, I admit it. I used Kas' body wash. To be fair, my

things had finally arrived, but since my place wouldn't be ready until after the weekend, I hadn't wanted to unpack anything. Or run out for anything.

The only thing I wanted to do was climb a certain sexy center and have all the dirty sex I could.

I kept telling myself it was because of the big brother cock blocking me for such a long drought. That it wasn't the way Kas' eyes followed me when I entered a room. Or how his gaze dipped down to my ass as he smirked.

Or the mind blowing orgasms he gave me. Over and over.

How cute he looked eating his Lucky Charms.

And forget about how he still pretended to not like Daisy, but was so excited about teaching her to play fetch, that he went through two bags of treats in a day and a half.

Nope. It was purely getting off on the regular for the first time in my life.

The clicking of the lock turning in the door cut off any more thoughts on the subject, and I grinned.

Because the bathroom door?

Left slightly ajar…

Yep, I might've wiped down the mirror just a few minutes ago so Kas wouldn't miss a single moment of seeing me get myself off thinking of him.

The game winning goal he scored with just 13 seconds to go in the third period? Le sigh.

The memory of how sexy he was on the ice, celebrating with his line and the rest of the team, sent a jolt of pleasure to my core. And there was no way I was going to break a routine.

Not even going there. Who wanted to be remembered as the girl who took away Kaspari Holken's mojo?

Not Jules Vaughn. No way. I'd seen Max deal with the puck bunnies my whole life, and steered clear of them until now.

My eyes caught a glimpse of him, dropping his bag as he noticed just where I was.

I soaped up the natural sponge Kas had a stockpile of in the linen closet (because, of course he did!), and ran it along my body. My arms. Across my collarbone.

My breasts. No shame in my game.

With a small smile, I let my hand smooth across my stomach, down to the apex of my thighs. Out of the corner of my eye, I saw Kas, standing, watching. His reflection in the mirror, sexy, dangerous, and everything I wanted right now.

When the sponge lightly touched my clit, a gasp fell from my lips. The door opened all the way, and Kas stormed in, eyes dark and demanding. "Cricket, I'm going to fuck you right here. Because I can't take another fucking moment of watching you touch yourself and not being able to do it myself."

He opened the glass door, pulling me into his arms in a crushing kiss.

"You're getting all wet," I murmured against his mouth, pressing up against him and not caring that I was getting his suit soaked.

"No," he rasped, "*you're* getting all wet. And I fucking love it."

His kiss became more and more demanding, until he murmured against my lips, "I'm going to fuck you against the counter, Cricket. Hard, fast, and without any fucking shame. I know you're ready for me. You loved knowing I was out there, didn't you?'

"Yes," I whispered, loving how the scruff along his jaw felt against my skin as his mouth worked its way down my neck. "Kas, I need you. I want you. Now."

He spun me until I faced the counter, caging me in with his arms as he pressed his erection against my ass. The material of his pants a delicious torture against my sensitive skin.

"Fuck, baby. Hold on tight, understand?"

I nodded, barely able to form a sentence.

His hand slid between us, lightly grazing my ass with his hand as he undid his zipper. The sounds told me he freed his cock, seconds before he pushed on my lower back, and nudged my legs apart before entering me in one quick and demanding thrust. I cried out at the intrusion, pushing my ass back up against him, demanding more.

I gasped at his relentless pace, my body ready to fall over the edge already from him watching me through the door. And if I admitted it, anticipating this moment all day long.

My inner walls started tightening, gripping his cock.

"Fuck, Cricket, I love how your pussy feels wrapped around my cock," he growled, taking me harder and further than I knew I could go.

His eyes caught mine in the mirror, and seeing him behind me, fucking me like only he could, tipped me over the edge. I cried out as I came, his hand on my shoulder as he punished me with each thrust into my body.

That made my world explode into a million pieces. With a final roar, he slammed into me one last time, and I felt his cum as he shuddered. Head resting on my shoulders.

We both stayed silent for a few moments, lingering in the post sex drunk, orgasmic bliss.

"Want to take another shower with me, Cricket?"

I giggled. "I'd love to, big guy."

CHAPTER FOURTEEN

KASPARI

Two months later...

"Come on, Cricket. Just move Daisy's things over, and get your ass permanently in my bed."

"Kas," she protested, as my lips trailed down her neck while she straddled me, pressing against my hard length. "You know, if Max finds out, you're dead."

I hissed out a breath, needing to be inside her, but knowing we had to leave for the arena soon. Game day ritual time. "Cricket, we're second in the division, two games out of first. And it's been two months, and you running back to your apartment to grab clothes or drag Daisy's crap back and forth is getting old, don't you think? Coach doesn't even have to know. Same building, same floor."

She bit her lip, grinding against my dick as I groaned. My hands gripped her hips and pulled her even more onto me, the thin cotton shorts Jules wore doing little to disguise how ready she was. "It's just down the hall. Is this really about that, or do you miss Daisy when she's not here?"

"Demon spawn and I have an understanding. I spoil her,

and you, and she tries not to be an asshole, even though she can't help herself."

Jules giggled, bouncing on my dick and not helping the situation. "She's not an asshole. Are you saying you're only nice to pussy so you can have my pussy?"

"Absofuckinglutely," I growled into her mouth before I kissed her.

BEEEEEEP BEEEEEEP

"Ugh," I cursed, kissing her and standing as she wrapped her legs around my waist. "Time to get to the rink, Cricket."

She pouted as she looped her arms around my neck. I carried her easily to my bedroom. With a smirk, I tossed her onto the bed. Her breasts bounced, and even wearing only my hoodie, she was a wet dream.

My wet dream.

"Let's get our Lucky Charms on, baby. Then come back and celebrate. I'm feeling really good about this game."

She wrinkled her nose, twisting her hair up onto the top of her head, the light brown strands in an artful bun wrapped with a scrunchie from her wrist. "It's the Pens, Kas."

"Yep."

"And Stahlski is still their goalie."

"And Vaughn is our coach now."

She crossed her legs, eyes tracking me as I grabbed my bag and threw in my usual game day stuff. "Aren't you even a least bit worried?"

"Nope. Hale will stay on top of any chirping or shit starting. And," I added as I tossed my bag on the bed and crawled towards her as she leaned back with a grin, "I doubt your brother is going to get on the ice to mess with me." I kissed her before she could protest. "I've got ten minutes, Cricket. Care to give me a little extra motivation?"

"Absofuckinglutely," she giggled as I covered her body with mine.

THE BUZZER SOUNDED, ending the game. Fuck, I was still on the rush from the last two minutes. Tied up until the literal last seconds, when the Pens pulled Stahlski in the last 45 seconds. After their line tried to block me from even getting a shot off, I finally saw an opportunity, and sent the puck sailing towards Hale. Who shot it across the center line to score an empty net goal.

Game winning assist, assholes.

Despite riding my ass still at every practice, Coach managed to join in on the celebration of my goal against his former team.

But the only person I wanted to celebrate with was nowhere in sight. As usual. Not only were we doing our best to keep what we had under wraps from the entire organization, but she hated the locker room and even sometimes left as soon as the game was over. And her obligations for the foundation were fulfilled.

Tonight, it was a family of four. The dad's face when they got to drop the puck and sit on the bench during warm-ups meant everything to me. Losing your mom, even in service to her country, left a huge hole to fill. A few of the guys and I offered to have them join us at this weekend's charity event as our guests. The kids, two boys and one girl, were so excited, but the dad's eyes said it all. Making them smile meant everything to him.

Hell if I wouldn't give him the chance as often as I could. I could almost hear my dad tell me how proud he was that I was using what God gave me and I busted my ass to do the good work.

All because of my Cricket.

I blew off the second half of the press conference with some lame excuse about returning my mom's phone call, which I did, obviously, but I needed her.

Cricket.

Changing as fast as I could, I took off towards where the Revenge Hype team usually gathered after a game, especially a win. Knowing she was most likely hanging with Sophia, her 'bestie', before she snuck back to my apartment.

And left the shower door open so I could watch her get herself off.

Half-mast time activated.

As I rounded the corner, I caught sight of her, hair in a high ponytail swinging as Sophia danced around her excitedly. She threw her head back, laughing, and I was gone.

Full hard-on.

Spinning around, she locked eyes with me and tilted her head towards the hallway that led to the storage and underground tunnels beneath the arena. One chin jerk and an adjustment later, I waited for her in the less bright concrete laden hallways.

"Damn, number 89, you were on fire. I thought the ice was going to melt," she murmured, leaping into my arms and climbing me like a spider monkey.

Turning, I pinned her between me and the wall, grinding my hips into the place my dick wanted to be. Kissing her, breathing in her scent. "You're a great incentive, Cricket." She gasped into my mouth, back arching, as her legs locked behind my back. "Fuck, we need to get home."

She giggled. "Miss your favorite pussy?"

I smirked. "I miss *both* my favorite pussies."

"WHAT THE ACTUAL FUCK?"

It was as if someone had dumped a bucket of ice water over the both of us. Frozen in place, as the one thing we'd successfully avoided finally hit us in the worse fucking way possible.

"Holken, get the fuck off my sister!"

I stepped back from Jules, gently setting her down on the floor, and moving her behind me. "Look, Vaughn-"

"Don't fucking even, Holken. I knew you were a fucking asshole, but this is bullshit." Max stalked toward us, finger pointing at me. "I knew I should've kicked your ass last year, and that first fucking practice. Going after my sister?"

Jules tried to step around me, but I held her back. "It's not like that, man."

"Don't fucking start, Jules," he barked. "Get your ass home. Now."

"That's it." Jules pushed my arm away and moved towards her brother. With the murderous on his face, probably wasn't a good idea. "Max, I am twenty-four years old. Not nine. Not anymore. And you have no say-"

"Get. Your. Ass. Home. Now." He grabbed her arm. "Do you not know what this asshole did last year? He could've fucking killed Stahlski's entire career with that hit." Arms up, he continued. "With his right side, he hit him there to win the fucking game. He used the injuries to his advantage. You don't go after the goalie, Jules. And I know what's best for you. Home. So I can kick this guy's ass."

"Maybe you should go, Jules." There was no way I was going to let her be put in the middle of this bullshit.

"Not even going to defend yourself, asshole? Is seducing my fucking sister a part of your plan?"

People looked our way from the end of the hall. If this escalated, it wasn't going to be pretty. For anyone.

Max yanked her arm, pulling her away from me. "Home. Now."

"Hey, let's not do this here. Because that game was intense, and the media is still hanging around, hoping to get more of the story," Sophia said in a low tone.

Max spun on her, dropping Jules' arm. "This guy's an asshole who goes after goalies. And is trying to fuck my little sister." He glared over his shoulder. "I'm going to do what I should've done last year. Kick his fucking ass."

"Maybe not now," Sophia said. "Coach. Those types of activities? Not a good idea. Especially after a big win like tonight. Get me? And," she added, "I'm pretty sure Jules can take care of herself."

"What the fuck, Sophia? Did you know about this?"

"Max, stop," Jules started.

He stepped in closer to me, jabbing his finger in my chest. "Stay the fuck away from my sister, asshole. You're benched. After I kick your ass.'

Sophia leaned against the wall like she was bored. "And you'll both be fucked, *Coach.*"

"I can't believe you, Max." Jules said, tears streaming down her face. "Please-"

"GET THE FUCK HOME, JULES. NOW." He roared, pointing down the hall where more people gathered. With a strangled cry, she spared me one last glance, before practically running away from all of us.

"Jules-" I stepped toward where she had gone, but Max stopped me.

"Stay the fuck away, and maybe I'll let you play again. Maybe."

I shrugged off his hand with a glare and brushed past him.

"Asshole, have you ever watched the tape? You do know Stahlski slid right when he checked up. You keep blaming him for something that never happened, *Coach* Vaughn. Dickhead." Sophia's voice carried, but I kept going.

But when I finally reached the main walkway, Jules was nowhere in sight.

CHAPTER FIFTEEN

JULES

"*A*nd you seriously haven't heard from him? At all?"

I shook my head, absently stroking Daisy's head as she curled up on my lap. "Not a peep since the note he left on my door the morning after. But it's not like I haven't been doing my best to avoid both of them, Soph." I let out a long sigh, crossing my legs on the bed as she ruffled through my closet. Daisy lifted her head and glared at me.

Oh, baby. I miss him, too.

I didn't even need to reread the note anymore. It sat in the top drawer of my dresser. Next to his hoodie, that no longer smelled like him.

I memorized it within two days.

Two long days of hoping. Two days of my big brother showing up for 'dinner' when I knew he was just checking to make sure Kas was staying far away.

Cricket,
I know you won't believe this, and probably think I'm just another asshole hockey player.

And you're right, I am. Because I thought I could keep you all to myself and we would just keep going on. Eating Lucky Charms together and my game would stay the same. But it wasn't fair to you. You deserve someone who doesn't sneak into dark hallways after games, or who takes you out for your favorite Italian.

And I can't let me come between you and your brother after what you've lost. Family is important.

So is the game. And I shouldn't make this any harder on you.

K.

Two weeks since that night.

Two long, lonely weeks of avoiding each other.

Of showing up at my office at the arena, and finding excuses to go out to the practice ice when the guys had practice only to see Max riding Kas and his line harder than the other guys. And I knew it was my fault.

Missing Lucky Charms.

And being so pissed at Max, I finally told him I was done with the way he treated me.

I was his sister. And he had to let me live my life.

With or without Kas.

Currently, it was without.

In fact, I was fairly certain Kas wasn't staying in his apartment. I overheard a few of the guys saying something about the wiring in his apartment being replaced. Which was utter bullshit, considering I had been there for months and charged my toy often.

But, if what they were saying was true about Max riding him nonstop at practice, since I stopped showing up after those first days, then maybe it was for the best.

I missed him. More than Daisy, which was saying a lot. Every time I opened the door when I came home, she darted out, mewing in front of his door.

"Your brother is an asshole. An overprotective, alpha male, Grade A asshole."

"Sophia!"

She spun around, her dark hair flying as she fluttered her hands. "It's true. He needs to get it through his thick skull that he can't boss around everyone and control things just because he wants to. People need their freedom, and be able to make the choices they want. Not what he wants." The bed bounced as she plopped down next to me, stretching out. Daisy glared at her in protest, but put her head back down as she went back to sleep.

"He doesn't know any other way. When our dad died, he had to take care of me and my mom. And somehow, play hockey." I stared up at the ceiling. "And the only reason I let him was because it finally made him smile again. When the Corps told us dad wasn't coming home, it was like a light went out. And I missed my brother." I turned my face to look at her. "I've never gone this long without talking to him, but I'm done letting him control my life."

She snickered. "I would have loved to see the look on his face when his key card didn't work."

Four days after the incident in the hallway, and three dinners later, I had Max change the code on my key card, and all the cards he gave me to enter the building. The silent treatment hadn't gotten through, so I changed tactics.

"The voicemails were brutal. But at least he got the point."

She ran her fingers along Daisy's back absently. "Do you love him?"

I thought about it. Did I?

I wasn't sure I could label what we had. All I knew was that he made me laugh. Loved when I tripped over things that weren't there. And gave me the best orgasms of my life.

And I missed eating Lucky Charms with him before games. I missed what we did after the game even more.

"I think so."

She sat up. "And do you want Max to realize you do?"

I sat up, too. "Yes. I want him to stop being...Max. And be my brother."

She pulled her phone out of the side pocket of the yoga leggings she wore.

My eyes narrowed suspiciously. "What are you doing?"

A finger in my face was my response as she spoke into her phone.

"Addie? It's Sophia. I need a favor." A giggle escaped her mouth, the bright red lipstick making her teeth look even whiter. "I need a team sweater with the number 89. And," she winked at me, 'Cricket Holken on the back, Yep, the entire thing, Work your magic, 'cause I need it for tonight. Really? I loooooove you. Yes, I will! You got it!"

"What did you just do?"

"I told you I would never let you get cock blocked. That also means getting my girl her man. And my Daisy needs her big, burly, grumpy hockey player," she said, scratching Daisy behind the ears. "So, what is the one thing the new WAG always does at her first home game as the girlfriend?"

I shrugged. "Wear his-" I clamped my hand over my mouth. "I couldn't."

"Grand gesture, baby. Huge statement. It says this guy is mine, and everyone else can fuck off."

Getting up on my knees, I nodded. "And it's so public, Max can't help but accept it."

Sophia mirrored my position. "He'll know you're serious."

"And so will Kas."

"And Daisy gets her Daddy back."

I wrinkled my nose. "Ew, don't say that. Daisy is a good girl."

Sophia cackled. "I'm sure you both are, bestie. Now get your ass in the shower. We have hockey players to manipulate."

FOR THE FIRST time since I was fifteen, I sat in the family section by the boards. Wearing a Seattle Revenge hockey sweater.

With CRICKET HOLKEN embroidered on the back for all the world to see.

Nervously awaiting the two men who needed to see it more than anyone else.

Sophia shoved a huge popcorn bucket into my hands as she stuffed two cans of White Claw into the cup holders on the armrests in between us.

"Aren't you working?"

"I do get two games off every other month if I want. And technically, I'm here. The girls have my cell. I'm not missing this for all the salsa in Chipotle."

I rolled my eyes. "I'm not sure how to take that."

"My love affair with salsa is nothing to scorn. You rank pretty fucking high if I say that. Okay, get ready, mama. Here they come."

The Revenge skated out onto the ice, along with the away team for warmups. My breath caught, nervous waves of nauseous hitting me.

Then I saw him. He looked the same, but sadder somehow. And I knew his game was still good, but not as great as it had been. Thankfully, the schedule had been light the past two weeks leading up to the stretch of games. But his eyes were less bright, the scruff along his jawline looked like he hadn't shaved in weeks. And I knew he hated beards.

He glanced up at me, as if he could feel me watching him.

I smirked. *Do you like to be watched, Kas, or is it just me?* I thought.

Just as he looked like he might turn away, Sophia hissed as she typed away on her phone, "Turn around, dumbass."

"Oh!"

I did, but while I looked up into the crowd, I heard a gasp from a few of the other WAGS and fans around us. Confused, I glanced at Sophia, who wore an evil grin. "What did you do?"

She gestured to the gigantic screen hovering over the ice rink. "Just using my job, so my bestie gets laid again."

When I looked over my shoulder, I saw the entire screen filled with the back of my jersey.

And everyone in the arena could clearly see the name and number I wore.

Including Max and Kas.

The arena erupted in cheers as Kas dropped his helmet and gloves and skated over to the boards.

"Get down there!'

I grinned at her and made my way over the two rows in front of us. Kas skidded to a stop, spraying ice everywhere.

"Hey," I yelled over the crowd, who were cheering even louder.

"You're wearing my number. And my name."

"I know."

He placed his hand on the glass. We stood staring at each other for what seemed like an eternity. "I miss you, Cricket."

"I never left, Kas. And you aren't allowed to either. Daisy and I need you."

He leaned his head on the plexiglass, then backed up so I could see him. "What about Max?"

"He'll have to learn to deal with it. With what I want. And I want you," I said simply.

"Oh, Cricket. It's much more than want. It's need. And fuck, I love you."

A huge grin broke across my face. "You do?'

He nodded. "I knew that I did the first time I saw you. And even more when you took my Lucky Charms."

"Even if I have a demon spawn?"

He nodded, his grin matching my own. "Even with the demon spawn. Who grew on me."

"Good. Because I love you, too. Now get the fuck out there, and win so we can get back our 'thing' big guy. I won't be responsible for messing up your game."

He slapped his palm against the plexi. "Hell yes, Cricket." He started to skate away backwards.

"Kas?" I called.

"Yes?"

"I'll catch you by the locker room after the game. No matter what."

As he skated over to his discarded equipment, and a grinning Hale and Coleman Sunders, I caught Max's eye over on the bench. He looked from me to Kas, then at the ground. When he looked up, he nodded at me.

And I knew, even though he would always be my big brother, he saw that there was someone in my life that I loved just as much as him.

And he would just have to deal with one of his players being the man of my dreams.

As for the game, let's just say, we celebrated all night long.

EPILOGUE

DAISY

"*L*isten here, you little demon spawn," Kas, the human my Jules loves almost as much as me, teased as he scooped me up and walked over the couch before snuggling up next to the person I love most in the world. "No more clawing at the door or mewing at all hours of the night."

If only he understood the flick of my tail was the equivalent of Jules' eyes roll.

All hours of the night? Exaggeration.

As it was, the two of them made the weirdest noises at the oddest times that worried me about their safety.

But, I knew my Jules could take care of anyone who came near Kas.

The way she rescued me, and took me home that day, showed me how amazing my new human was.

I still worried about the two of them, regardless. Besides being my humans, they played and petted and gave the best treats.

For a kitten barely five months old, these things are

important. Just like the blanket on the couch, all fluffy in ways that made me dream of my mama.

I had to keep an eye on them, Silly humans could barely see that they were made for one another.

Who else took care of them like I did?

Especially when they came home twittering about hat tricks (hats do not do tricks, silly humans, unless the ghosts they never saw but I watched all the time were bored), locking me out or locking me in the cat nap room.

And the noises were enough that I needed to check if they were ok, because not only did they feed me, but Kas was superb at throwing my favorite toy over and over.

So easily trained, and always so happy when I gave it to him to throw. He might play with a stick, but his aim was flawless.

I knew he liked me, despite his grumblings.

"Kas," Jules admonished, reaching over to rub me behind my ears and cooing at me. "She's not a demon spawn. And let's not forget that you keep sneaking her tuna behind my back, as if I wouldn't notice."

"At least she doesn't steal all my Lucky Charms," he grumbled, kissing her nose as she giggled.

I loved my Jules. From the first moment I saw her, I knew she was mine, and we would take care of each other.

And then, he rescued us from the crazy water that started pouring down when I was all alone.

That whole idea about cats not liking water? I don't know if it was true before that happened to me, but it is now. When my humans shower, I stay far away.

A shiver raked down my back, and Kas hummed as he rubbed under my chin.

From that moment on, he was ours. Yes, I totally take credit. I licked my paw, then purred with appreciation.

I loved Jules, but I knew she was lonely. And her brother, Max?

Not a fan.

I also fully admit that hissing at him and seeing him jump back brought me more joy than my favorite crinkly cellophane cat toy.

Jules giggled as I settled on Kas' chest. "She only steals them when you're not looking."

I totally did.

"No she doesn't."

She nodded, snuggling up alongside him as they started the movie. "She does."

And he knows. The marshmallows get stuck in my teeth, but the rainbow ones are my favorite.

"Don't worry, Daisy," he whispered, eyeing Jules as she giggled. "Our deal stands. Hiss at Max, as many marshmallows as you want, my little demon spawn."

"Stop," Jules gasped for breath. "You two are going to have to figure out how to get along, especially this Christmas," she added, still breathless from laughing, eyes sparkling.

"Don't worry, Cricket. I'll turn on my smolder, and everything will work itself out. Now watch your movie before I take matters into my hands. And by my own hands, I mean my hands and you're going to be the matter I take."

Another reason I loved my Kas?

He loved Tangled almost as much as Jules.

Though I did catch him watching The Little Mermaid a few days ago.

Sigh. That Prince Eric.

But no one will replace my Smolder. Sigh. Lucky Rapunzel.

Except for my Kas.

. . .

NEED MORE? Subscribe to my newsletter here to get an exclusive peek at what happens coming this Christmas between Kas and Max...and maybe Sophia will be around, making sure her bestie is well taken care of.

F*** on the Ice Rink

SPICY PUCK

ARIANA ST. CLAIRE

Loved Kas and Jules (and of course, Daisy!!)? Consider leaving a review!

WANT A PEEK AT KELLAN AND HIS
DAUGHTER, WHO FALLS FOR HIS
BEST FRIEND? KEEPING READING, &
THEN GET STEAL MY KISS <u>HERE</u>!

SHE WAS OFF LIMITS. TOO BAD SHE
WAS ALREADY MINE.
AND MY BEST FRIENDS DAUGHTER.

CHAPTER ONE

ANTHONY

"Luc, I'm fine, promise. Just needed a few days away from… everything." I exhaled, praying he would take the hint. I loved my nephew. Who was more of a younger brother to me. The little shit shouldered more responsibility for everyone else than he should. "And your father."

At least the little shit who tried to fuck him over landed himself in jail, and awaited trial for blackmail, among other chargers.

Silver lining?

Coming home, after all the hell I'd inadvertently put him through, led him to the woman he loved more than anything.

Even if she was the daughter of my big brother's fiercest rival.

Actually, that part was pretty badass, if not karma doing its job.

I hung up, placing my phone on the distressed bartop and motioned the bartender for another bourbon.

I couldn't escape racing even here. At the beach, not a track or race car in sight. The roar of the engines didn't follow me. But Falling Leaves Bourbon from Gentry

Distillery was my drink of choice. And Luc's primary sponsor for Anders Racing.

Which was how I fucked up his life instead of manning up and taking responsibility for my actions. Even if I had done nothing wrong, it cost him his seat overseas in the most prestigious open wheel series in the world.

I glanced around the sleek beachside cantina attached to the hotel I was staying at for the weekend. At the bartop, worn not by years of use, but by some guy who probably sold it for ten times its worth. The place gave off a classic yet low key beach vibe with a view of the ocean. From the open-air patio, waves crashed gently against the shore, lit by the full moon. It was a clear night, and I was hell bent on drowning my misery in bourbon despite the gorgeous scenery.

And wishing the corner had an old school jukebox that took quarters

Then my view instantly changed to the absofuckinglutely best thing I've seen.

A waterfall of blonde hair, followed by a body that demanded my attention, peeked over the bar a few stools down from me. And I stared in her direction, my mouth watering at the sight of her.

Holy. Shit.

Lightning struck my fucking cock, and I found myself, drink in hand, swiveling in her direction. She was a gravitational pull. All light and full of life.

I was helpless to resist, even though every molecule screamed I shouldn't. The weight of my actions weighed heavily, and fuck if for one night I wanted to leave it all behind.

Too bad the thought hit me like a ton of bricks alongside a blonde bombshell. The possibility of being told to fuck off? High.

I almost felt close to my old self. Except there was an

inexplicable force drawing me to her. When she turned her aqua eyes on me after finally getting the bartender's attention, my cock stood at full attention.

The way her pupils dilated as she sized me up, starting at my feet and working her way up, made me wonder how she sounded when she came.

God, I wanted to know. As did my rock hard dick.

Her lips did that thing, pursing and becoming a major distraction, as she thought whether to deck me or kiss me. I was betting on the latter.

As was my dick.

With my luck lately, the former was in the lead, and coming around the final chicane.

Even when I tried, I couldn't get the fuck away from racing. It was in my blood. Especially the blood rushing to a place other than my brain currently. The buzz from the bourbon was in full effect, and liquid courage gave me the balls to actually talk to her. Thank fuck whiskey dick happened after a few more.

She hit the brakes on all my plans, eyes darkening and licking her fuck-me-red lips. The smile she shot me was a mixture of star-filled nights and not so innocent desire. "I need a distraction. And you're the man for the job."

"Excuse me?" I smirked, amused, and turned on. My eyes traced along the lines of her body, and I licked my lips before making my way back up to her captivating aqua eyes. Fuck, I wanted to ruin her perfectly applied make up.

Her laugh was husky and like honey dripping down on a summer evening. Evoking all kinds of late night fantasies. Bending her over. Backing her luscious ass up against a wall while we indulged in a forget all our troubles dirty fuck. "What? I'm offering you a pickup line free opening, and you don't want to take it?"

"Oh, gorgeous, I have no problem taking what I want." I

downed the rest of my drink with a smirk. She locked her gaze on mine and threw hers back without hesitation.

Gold spun silk brushed her bare shoulder as she canted her head with a small grin. "Really? And do you see something," she murmured, a challenge in her eyes, "You like?"

I moved closer, invading her space with a smirk.. So close she had to tilt her head back to maintain eye contact and I could smell her shampoo. "Absolutely. When I find something I want or crave, it's mine." I leaned in, growling the last word in her ear. My dick, happy to be back doing our usual routine, strained against the zipper of my pants. "Until I get what I want."

And fuck, did I want her.

Sick of the melancholy feeling I owed an explanation for my every move. Except for my nephew, Luc. Who never asked for anything. He was always the one taking care of everyone else.

Including me.

That was pretty fucked up.

My big brother's kids were the one thing he didn't mess up. Luc, Bri, and Nick were the reason I came back to stay. They were the one bright spot in a messed up situation.

So, I took off for the weekend. To take a break from the world.

I walked into the hotel bar, feeling far too fucking old and wanting to be alone.

Seek solace in the bottom of a glass when she struck like lightning on a humid North Carolina summer night.

Damned if I craved nothing more in the world right now than to fuck this glorious woman. Lose myself in her. Pupils dilated as her eyes darted to my mouth, and she licked her lips. Igniting thought after filthy thought of the things I could do.

My eyes slowly raked down her body. To her feet, which

were in the sexiest pair of heels I'd ever seen in my life. High, with a tiny black bow that drove me crazy. Her legs were never ending, leading up to an ass that had my dick at attention.

Stunning little vixen.

Undeniably sexy and yet innocent.

Hard and dirty, without stopping until she screamed my name like a dirty prayer. Breaking apart, over and over. Raw, and filling her with my cum until she couldn't take anymore, passed out in my arms.

Sated.

A sheen of sweat covering our naked bodies.

A growl rumbled deep in my throat at the thought, causing her to shiver and let out a whimper, as though she could sense my thoughts..

The dirtier, the better.

She glanced around the room, and said, "Can't even play a song on the jukebox to set the mood. "

"Jukebox, huh?"

"Music sets the mood for everything."

"Agreed." She eyed me over the rim of her glass. Taking her time as I continued. "And no one makes mix tapes anymore."

"Mix tapes, huh? Did you create the perfect soundtrack for someone?"

I shrugged. "Once or twice. It's a lost art. Not unlike... telling a girl she's beautiful and wanting to buy her a drink. And meaning it because she's stunning, and her smile knocks you out. Just because."

"Beautiful? But," she added with a shrug, licking her lips, demeanor changing as she made a decision. "What if I need something or someone? Just for tonight? To make me forget or," she paused, tilted her as her hair fell forward. A tendril brushing her breast like a lover's caress. "Have a night I'll never forget?"

"Well," I breathed, inching closer, "I'll make sure you get *whatever* you need or want. What both of us want."

As I pinned her against the wood top with my body, she let out a sharp inhale..

Strawberries and sunshine filled my nose as I nuzzled the sensitive area behind her ear. A predator stalking his prey. Leading her right into my bed.

"Little vixen. The things I want to do? Show you? Will never. Leave. You. You'll still feel me, everywhere I've been, for a very long time."

The silence between us was louder than the pointless conversations and ill-timed pick-up lines. Blanketing us in a sensual fog that was thick and so damn tempting I couldn't resist her pull.

"Tell me you live close?" she asked, grabbing her purse from the bar. Breathless and needy.

I chuckled darkly. "Very. About four floors up."

Hotel bars were convenient as fuck when you were drunk and ended up alone. Or drunk enough to invite a beautiful woman to your room. Try to get the front desk called on you because she screamed your name loud enough for the people across the hall to hear.

The scent of strawberries and sunshine hit me as she tilted her head. Her cheek brushed mine, pushing the limits of my control. "Perfect."

Taking her hand in mine and tossing a fifty on the bar with the other, I led her quickly to the lobby elevators. The clicking of her heels on the floor, a staccato beat pulsing through our bodies like a rhythm we couldn't deny.

Her whole body vibrated with sexual tension, but she waited for the doors to open. And watched me in antic-ipation.

Unable to hold back, I captured her head in my hands, angling it just the way I wanted. Touched her lips with mine, running my tongue along the seam of her lips as she trembled. Enjoying the soft fullness and picturing how they would look around my cock. "I bet your panties are wet for me, and your pussy is just begging to be filled, isn't it?"

She melted, her lush curves teasing my cock through my pants. Lips eager, and her tongue entwined with mine. Dancing sensual and dirty with an urgency I couldn't deny much longer.

The way a fucking kiss should be.

Taking. Giving. Wanting. Craving. Consuming.

With a whimper, she pulled back. My little vixen whispered against my mouth, "Very, and God, yes."

Hell yes.

The elevator doors slid open, and we stumbled in, grabbing and groping like two teenagers. Until I touched her ass, firm and toned. Fuck me.

Her back arched, pressing every curve against me. Tempting and more than I deserved. I planned on taking everything and anything I could tonight.

And fuck the consequences.

Like I used to.

One last time.

ACKNOWLEDGMENTS

You know those little moments that add up to big moments that are kismet?

From a crazy cover image, to a kitten that was a boy but really is a girl, to a favorite cereal…

It all ended up just the way it was supposed to in the end. But, it's only the beginning.

Sarwah, thank you. For letting me switch out my guy, to all those messages and laughs. I appreciate you so much!!

To my amazing alphas! Omg, I don't know what I would've done without you. Jas, Lakshmi, and Gabs!! The three of you make me love writing with every message, comment, and I adore you.

Wolf, thank you for making all my book boyfriends come to life. Marshmallows and all…

My Good Girls team, you have shared tears, laughter, Damon, our favorite moments, and are the most wonderful women I've ever had the absolute pleasure to get to know. From listening to teasers (I know, so difficult!!! BWUAHA-HAHA!) to letting me bounce silly ideas off you, and sharing your love for our boyfriends, and reminding me of all the good things when the days feel hard. I love you all. Thank you from the bottom of my heart for joining me on this journey!!

To my boys. I love you, and your hugs are the best part of my day. Thank you for letting me do all the things that sometimes drag me away and reminding me that our time is still the best part of everything!! I love you both so much. More, most, mostest, and then some.

To my husband. Simply put, A&F. Thank you for wanting a gray kitten. There aren't enough words or pages for me to tell you all the things. I love you.

Mila. I know you started out life with us as Milo, but everything fell into place just as it was meant to, my crazy kitten. We love you, and Daisy would have never happened without you.

To my readers. Thank you. So freaking much. My heart is all warm and fuzzy, because you helped me go from chasing my dream to owning it. You're amazing, and to think of how many people have realized their dreams because of readers is humbling. You are the best!

ABOUT THE AUTHOR

Ariana can be found getting her Zen on while practicing hot yoga, going for a run, reading her favorite authors in the middle of the night, or having a bourbon on a Saturday while plotting the lives of her characters as they whisper and sometimes yell in her ear.

She lives her own Happily Ever After with her amazing husband, who shares her love of racing, comic books, and Firefly, along with her two spirited also amazing boys who love reading books under a blanket just as much as she does.

ALSO BY ARIANA ST. CLAIRE

REVVED UP SERIES

When We Were Prequel (newsletter exclusive! Click to subscribe)

Track Me Down Duet Part One

Turn Me Loose Duet Part Two

Never Have I Ever (A NYE Bonus Scene)

Mistletoe Madness (Christmas Party Shared World) Nov. 28, 2023

Be My Secret Santa (A Stranger Session Christmas/Res & Piper prequel)

Claim My Heart (Van & Gia) A Revved Up Standalone
Coming 2024

STRANGER SESSIONS

When We Were Prequel

Trust Fall

Free Fall

DAD'S BEST FRIEND/REVVED UP STANDALONE

Steal My Kiss

SEATTLE REVENGE

Spicy Puck (F*** on the Ice Rink)

(Pucked Up Short) 12/2023

(Puck Dating) 4/1/2/2024

(Pucker Up Romance) 7/15/2024

HURTSBORO HUMMINGBIRDS

Touch Me Down

ALOHA HAWAII RELIEF SERIES/REVVED UP

Lei Me Down

Surf My Heart

Love Beach

Summer with a Country Star (July 2024)